DEADLINE DAWN

A Play

ANTHONY BOOTH

SAMUEL   FRENCH

LONDON
NEW YORK TORONTO SYDNEY HOLLYWOOD

ISBN 0 573 02347 6

MADE AND PRINTED IN GREAT BRITAIN BY
LATIMER TREND & COMPANY LTD PLYMOUTH

MADE IN ENGLAND

DEADLINE DAWN

Leila, the leader of the operation
Tariq, the hit-man
Naomi Nathan, the hostage
Brother Luis, the priest

The action of the play takes place in an attic room of a tenement building in a Middle East city

Time: the present

PRODUCTION NOTES

This work must be played hard and savagely and none of the language or business must be toned down. There are many compelling pauses in the play which must not be hurried.

Before rehearsing this play it is a good idea to read it, then read it again, so that you understand fully these characters and what makes them what they are.

Leila is the modern product of the terrorist régime but despite her protestations about the fate of her sister one has the feeling that she really does this because she likes doing it. Although she cannot do without Tariq she hates him because he is so uncouth, the very opposite to her and although she is domineering as far as he is concerned she is basically frightened of of him. She knows that Tariq would not hesitate to kill her if the occasion arose. Tariq is an animal who has survived through toughness and cunning. He has no feelings, no loyalties and murder is something to be shrugged off. As a member of the old school of terrorists and no longer a young man, he deeply resents a young woman being put in charge of this operation over him.

Luis is an enigmatic character. He must not be portrayed as a holy man. He could be and must be depicted as a man who has chosen to wear a monk's habit because it is comfortable and useful, yet despite this he must have the quiet dignity of a priest. He is of no particular order and one gets the impression that he drifts wherever he wishes and does what he can to help others wherever he happens to be. Naomi is a young intelligent woman who is naturally very frightened under the circumstances but she does, despite this, carry a certain dignity and courage.

Regarding the dress, Leila wears olive or light green trousers tucked into ankle-length boots with a matching tunic top. It is almost a uniform. She is neat and her clothes are clean which enables her to walk unnoticed through the city. Tariq, on the other hand, is quite the opposite. He is dirty and unshaven and is uncouth. He wears a sweat-soaked khaki shirt with dirty rumpled trousers to match and rough boots. A worn cartridge bandolier slung over one shoulder enhances the outfit but is not necessary. Luis wears a plain roomy monk's habit and sandals with a white cord round his waist. He does not carry a crucifix or show anything to depict a particular denomination. Originally we made this from two old matching army blankets and the result was ideal. Naomi wore a light cotton dress and a half-slip which tore very easily. In actual fact she made a slip out of an old white sheet which was ripe and tore very easily.

The guns used were reproductions which gave authenticity and were credible when they were put down as one heard the thud. As they didn't fire, Tariq, at the end of the play concealed a small starter-pistol on the upstage side of his machine-gun and fired that twice. It was done very quickly and no-one noticed. The same pistol can be used off stage for the other shots when Tariq is wounded and Naomi is killed.

Light the stage with as much lighting from the *side* as possible, from the window, and use spots if possible rather than foots and battens for the acting areas.

The theme music of the play is the Adagio movement from the "Concerto de Aranjuez" by Rodrigo.

Anthony Booth

The room is virtually bare. Downstage left is an open door. Above that is an open window (or alcove) above that upstage is another opening which is used by Tariq as a look-out.

Downstage right there are some dirty sacks on which Naomi lies. Above them is an old wooden box or beer crate which Luis uses as a seat. There is a similar box by the look-out used by Tariq.

At the window there is a rough small trestle table angled out into the room on which is a small canvas satchel which contains a small walkie-talkie set and a hand-grenade. Also on the table is an army water-bottle and a small transistor radio.

The room is dirty, odd pieces of rubbish lie around, even in the soft shadows of the evening light it is a cold, unloved place.

SCENE 1

As the CURTAIN *rises Naomi Nathan, a woman of about twenty-eight, is discovered half lying on the dirty sacks, right. She is dishevelled having been roughly abducted from the street. Her attitude is a mixture of proud defiance and abject despair*

Sitting on the box up left is Tariq. He is a man of indefinite age. Tariq is hard, revoltingly crude and utterly ruthless. He cradles a sub-machine-gun easily which he rarely puts down. He gazes out left, keeping watch on the roof of the next building

Below the table left but facing up stage is Leila. She is about thirty. She is the brains of the outfit and like Tariq, if cornered, can be quite ruthless, yet enigmatically she has a quality of compassion and can be vulnerable

The first twenty seconds of the play are played in silence broken only by the music which comes from the transistor set. It is the Adagio movement from the "Concerto de Aranjuez" by Rodrigo

Tariq is obviously irritated and he suddenly moves down to the table to switch off the set. As his hand touches it, Leila speaks

Leila (*curtly*) Leave it.
Tariq Switch that goddam——
Leila (*sharply*) I said leave it, Tariq!
Tariq (*angrily*) But supposing they want to get in touch with us?
Leila (*evenly*) That is their problem.

He stares at her belligerently for a moment then, turning his head slightly to his right, spits in contempt. He shrugs then casually returns to the box and sits again, gazing out. Leila lifts the water-bottle from the table. She is about to drink then changes her mind. She glances left towards the girl and this is the first time we see her face. She crosses right to the girl and stops above her, right. She hands her the water-bottle. The girl doesn't notice

  (*Quietly*) Take some.

The girl looks up slowly then takes it. She drinks greedily then without looking at Leila hands it back. Leila wipes the mouthpiece, takes a short sip then replaces the cork. She returns casually to the table and puts the water-bottle on it then switches off the radio. She gazes out of the window apparently lost in thought. There is a long pause, broken suddenly by Tariq

Tariq (*impatiently*) Why the hell don't they contact us? It's four hours now.
Leila Four hours is nothing.
Tariq (*annoyed*) To you maybe but I want action.
Leila (*evenly*) Then you'll have to wait.

Tariq moves down angrily

Tariq (*angrily*) If I was running this——

She turns to him

Leila (*curtly*) It would end in a bloodbath.
Tariq Maybe, but that is the only thing they understand . . . a show of force . . . results. (*He moves very slightly towards the girl*) They would soon know we mean business if we shot a few hostages.
Leila That's your answer to everything, isn't it?
Tariq It's the only answer.
Leila (*firmly*) You are wrong.
Tariq (*almost shouting*) Wrong! Don't give me that bullshit, it's the only way, I tell you! This is a man's job, they should never have sent a bloody woman.

Leila turns on him. She is coldly angry and moves right to him

Leila (*furiously*) Now listen to me, I don't take that from anybody, least of all a crude bastard like you. If you had any intelligence you would realize that this is the only way to handle this. (*She breaks off and moves across him gazing at the girl. She spells it out for him*) In her we have something to bargain with and while there is some hope of saving her life, they will pull every trick to get round it. But whatever they offer the result is the same, Suleman Persha for her. (*She turns to him*) If you handled this you would destroy any sympathy for our cause, we should be branded as assassins throughout the world.

Tariq (*angrily stubborn*) But we should have done something positive.

Leila And died stupidly for nothing. (*She moves to him, speaking quietly now*) Do you want to die, Tariq?

He does not answer

I don't . . . (*Quietly*) We'll play it my way.

He stares at her hard for a moment then turning his head slightly to the left he spits in contempt. She doesn't react in any way. He turns and wanders back to his box where he sits, staring at her broodingly. After a moment she moves to above right of the girl, half-kneels on one knee and touches her lightly on one shoulder. The girl cringes away from the contact

(*Quietly*) I'm sorry it had to be you.

Naomi (*half contemptuously*) Sorry!

Leila Yes, it was never our intention. The target was your father, the Ambassador. Unfortunately his bodyguard was too quick for us and in snatching him away, exposed you. In some ways it gives us a stronger hand.

Naomi I don't see how.

Leila Your father loves you very much?

Naomi He lives for me and the children.

Leila stands, staring down at Naomi

Leila Exactly. He will be desperate to gain your release. The Israeli Government might well dispense with an elderly ambassador, but they may consider very carefully the loss of one of its young countrymen.

Naomi Why should they?

Leila Because they might not wish to risk world opinion if you die.

Naomi rolls on to her knees gazing at Leila in disbelief

Naomi You mean you would kill me?

Leila (*evenly*) If necessary, yes.

Naomi (*angrily*) What are you people, animals?

Tariq is furious, he comes down quickly, pointing his gun at her

Tariq (*angrily*) We'll soon show you.

Leila moves across so that she is between them

Leila (*sharply*) Keep out of this, Tariq.

Tariq (*angrily*) I won't take that from a bitch like this.

Naomi (*her voice rising*) You'll have to. If you kill me you won't have anything to bargain with, or didn't that enter your thick skull . . . ?

Tariq lifts his gun quickly, almost as if he is going to fire. He is furious

Tariq Why, you dirty little——

Leila (*very sharply*) That's enough.

Tariq reluctantly lowers his gun

(*Calmly*) You have a point. However, there is nothing in the rules about roughing you up.

Naomi And I wouldn't put that past either of you, especially him.

Leila (*easily*) It's up to you then, isn't it?

Naomi (*with spirit*) It's easy to make the rules when you have the whip hand. Anyone can be brave and bluster when they are armed and no-one can do anything about it.

Leila That argument is all too easy. What you don't seem to remember is that there are only three of us, Tariq, myself and Shumac on the floor below.

Naomi And me with nothing.

Leila While outside there are upwards of two hundred troops.

Tariq moves back to his box, keeping watch out of the window

All the streets are cordoned off for three blocks to prevent our escape and there are snipers on every roof ready to kill without any hesitation.

Naomi (*loudly*) And I'd do the same if I had the chance.

Leila You would?

Naomi Without hesitation.

Leila I wonder.

Naomi You don't believe me?

Leila No, I don't think I do.

Naomi (*dully*) There is no point, anyway.

Leila Oh, but there is. (*She crosses behind Naomi to near centre,* *then turns to speak to her*) If you could dispose of us, bearing in mind that you would almost certainly die yourself, would you be prepared to do it?

Naomi (*stubbornly*) Yes.

Leila It is easy to kill but it takes a peculiar kind of courage to take one's own life.

Naomi I could do it.

Leila I don't believe you.

Naomi Try me.

Leila stares at her for a moment then makes a decision

Leila Very well. (*She crosses to the table, takes a hand-grenade from the canvas bag, then returns to Naomi. She shows her the grenade*) You have seven seconds after you have drawn the pin and released the spring.

Naomi (*shortly*) I know how to use a hand-grenade.

Leila (*slowly*) Then this is it then, isn't it?

Tariq, for the first time shows fear, he starts to move down to Leila

Tariq Leila, for God's sake . . .!

Leila (*quietly*) Quiet, Tariq.

Tariq Are you mad!

Leila Seven seconds.

Leila tosses the grenade on the sacking in front of Naomi. Tariq steps forward to try and retrieve it but Leila puts up an arm to restrain him. Naomi stares at the grenade almost fascinated

You have seven seconds to live once you have pulled the pin.

For a few seconds they stare at each other. Tariq moves above Naomi with his gun trained on her ready to cut her down if necessary. Naomi suddenly makes up her mind. She snatches up the grenade, stands, then turns away to pull the pin. She tries but at the last minute finds she cannot bring herself to do it. She drops the grenade then throws herself down on the sacks, weeping in frustration. Tariq lowers his gun with relief

Tariq (*quietly*) Jesus!

Leila, who has stood quite unmoved throughout, stares at the weeping girl for a few seconds, then picks up the grenade, checking to see that the pin is safely home

Leila (*quietly*) It isn't that easy after all, is it?

She returns to the table and replaces the grenade in the bag. As she does so there is the sound of someone kicking an empty tin in the passage off left. She reacts like lightning. Snatching up her gun she springs to slightly below the door, her legs spreadeagled, her body crouched, and holds the gun outstretched with both hands. Tariq, up centre, also covers the door with his gun

Luis (*off*) Don't fire, I'm unarmed.
Leila (*slowly*) Whoever you are, come in very slowly with your hands on your head.

There is a pause, then Luis enters just inside the door

(*Curtly*) That's far enough.

Luis stands there without moving. He is thick-set and wears a rough monk's habit and old sandals. He carries a small linen roll in his right hand

How did you get in?
Luis Your guard allowed me to enter after he had searched me. He followed me as far as the door here.
Leila What's that in your hand?
Luis Food.
Leila Put it on the table, very slowly.

Luis moves to the table and puts the material down, lowering his hands to do so

Keep one hand on your head.

He does so

Now tip the contents on to the table, slowly.

He lifts a corner of the material letting the contents—some meat-rolls—fall out

Leila Right, stand aside.

Luis moves back a little from the table

Tariq!

Tariq moves to the table and examines the food briefly, then shrugs

Tariq Nothing.

Leila Get down on the floor on your hands and knees.

Luis does so. Leila nods to Tariq. Tariq puts his gun down within easy reach on the floor then quickly and expertly runs his hands over Luis' body to see if he is armed

Tariq He's clean.

Tariq quickly retrieves his gun, covering Luis

Leila Get up and move over there. (*She points towards Naomi*)

Luis gets up and moves to Naomi, who is half crouched on the sacks. He half-kneels beside her

Luis (*gently*) Are you all right?

Naomi nods

Leila (*curtly*) Shut up, I'll tell you when to speak.

Leila crosses to centre, she surveys Luis for a moment, intrigued. She still covers him with her gun, backed up by Tariq, upstage

Now, who are you and what the hell are you doing here?

Luis (*evenly*) My name is Luis and I have come to offer myself as hostage in place of Mrs Nathan here.

Leila You!

The absurdity of the situation appeals to her. She laughs quite openly. Luis gets up and moves to her a little

Luis What is so funny?

Leila You. What possible value could you have as a hostage?

Luis Humanitarian grounds.

Leila My poor deluded priest, get your values right. Who's brilliant idea was this, anyway?

Luis (*simply*) My own. I thought there was a better chance of someone like myself to act as a go-between.

Leila Your cloth wouldn't have saved you. Shumac has a very sensitive trigger finger, he invariably shoots first then challenges. You were very lucky, you will never know how lucky you were.

Luis (*simply*) My life is of little importance.
Leila To us, but not to you. So, you risked your life to bring us food?
Luis Not you. Her.

Leila half smiles to herself. She crosses below them to right of them

Leila Ah, chivalry. (*She turns to them, speaking sharply*) Now let's have the truth.
Luis I also have a message from the Minister of Internal Security.
Leila They are going to release Persha?
Luis He didn't discuss anything with me. He asked me to tell you that they will lower a field telephone from the roof in a few minutes. They are waiting for me to appear at the window to know when to drop it.
Tariq (*quickly*) It's a trick.
Luis There is no trick, it is the only practical means of contact between yourself and the authorities.

Leila crosses casually to the door, summing up the situation. She turns and surveys Luis for a moment

Leila All right, give them the signal.

Luis crosses to the window, hesitates for a moment, then steps right up to it and slowly raises his hand

Right, now get back to the girl.

Luis returns to Naomi who is now standing, watching. He puts an arm protectively round her shoulders. After a few seconds the field telephone appears from above, dangling on a light line. It hangs, swaying slightly. Leila beckons to Naomi

Come here.

Naomi glances at Luis almost for instructions. He releases her, nodding slightly. She goes to the table, hesitantly

Now take hold of the line and bring it into the room.
Naomi Why?
Leila Because I am the obvious target of any sniper. If they recognize you in time they won't fire. Now bring it in.

Luis (*half stepping jorward, urgently*) Don't risk her life, let me do it.

Tariq motions him back with his gun

Wait for God's sake. If they do shoot her by mistake you will have nothing to bargain with.

Tariq (*quickly*) He's got a point.

Leila turns on Tariq

Leila (*curtly*) I'm in charge, not you!

They face each other for a few seconds

Tariq You had better be right.

Leila, after a momentary pause, turns to the girl

Leila Go to the window slowly, let them see you, then pull the phone in.

As Naomi does this they all watch tensely. As she puts the telephone on the table she turns to Leila. Leila looks at Tariq with a slight smile. Tariq spits and turns away. She speaks to the girl

Now get over there again.

Naomi returns to Luis. Leila stares at the telephone, apparently lost in thought. After a moment Tariq speaks

Tariq (*irritably*) Well, aren't you going to contact them?

Leila No.

Tariq Why not, for God's sake?

Leila (*evenly*) Because they know my terms, it's up to them to contact me.

Tariq stares at her for a moment, then moves quickly to above the table

Tariq If you want to play the heroine that's O.K., but it's my bloody neck you are risking, too. (*He puts his hand on the telephone*)

Leila (*coldly quiet*) Take your hand off.

Tariq (*furiously*) Who the bloody hell do you——

Leila (*very sharply*) I said off!

Her tone makes him hesitate but he still keeps his hand on the telephone. She slowly points her automatic at him, she will kill him if necessary and he knows it

(*Dangerously quiet*) I mean it, Tariq.

He slowly withdraws his hand and moves away. He turns as if to speak but changes his mind. He spits contemptuously then settles on his box glaring at her. There is quite a pause then he trains his gun automatically on Luis and Naomi and Leila unties the rope from the telephone

Luis Are you all right?

Naomi (*wearily*) Yes . . . yes, I'm all right.

Luis I wish there was something I could do.

Naomi (*turning to him*) What made you come, anyway?

Luis I don't know. It all seemed so ineffectual. Everyone just standing there, waiting. No-one seemed to be doing anything constructive.

Naomi (*turning away wearily*) What can they do?

Luis I don't know but there seems to be no sense of urgency, I felt I had to do something so I came.

Naomi And they let you?

Luis They threatened to shoot me if I entered the building.

Naomi (*turning to him*) But you still came.

Luis Yes . . . I can't explain it but I had this tremendous compulsion.

Naomi That was brave of you.

He turns away a little and moves slightly across towards the window

Luis No, I knew they wouldn't fire, it was only a gesture on their part. I had the feeling that they were glad that at last someone was at least doing something positive.

Naomi (*gently grateful*) Thank you.

He moves back to her a little

Luis As things stand, there seems little point now.

Naomi You weren't to know that. (*Pause*) Did you speak to my father?

Luis No, I was on the fringe of the crowd next to the barrier but as I crossed the road, he called out to me.

Naomi Yes?

Luis He said, "Tell her we are doing everything we can and the children are safe".

Naomi (*softly*) Thank God for that.

Leila Why? We would not have harmed them. We have no quarrel with children.

Luis (*forcefully*) You have no quarrel with this girl either. Let her go, I beg of you. I will willingly take her place.

Leila A noble gesture, priest, but an empty one.

He stares at her for a moment before speaking

Luis I brought her some food, may I give her some?

Leila nods to Tariq who comes to the table and picks up a roll with meat in it. He opens the roll, looks at the meat, then laughs

What is so funny?

Tariq moves to centre a little

Tariq You know what you've brought her? A pork sandwich.

Luis What is wrong in that?

Tariq What's wrong? She's an Israeli, and you bring her pork?

Luis If you are so ignorant there is no point in explanation.

He turns his back on Tariq, facing upstage. Tariq is annoyed, he moves to him

Tariq Oh no, tell me, we've nothing else to do, it will fill in the time and then we can all have a good laugh.

Luis (*contemptuously quiet*) An ignorant man like you wouldn't understand.

Tariq (*truculently*) Try me.

Leila (*curtly*) Leave it alone, Tariq.

Tariq (*belligerently*) No, he called me ignorant, all right then, he's got to tell me.

Luis turns to him. He speaks quietly as if explaining something to a small child

Luis Very well. You make the mistake of mixing the Jewish religion with the State of Israel. Israel is a polyglot nation full of Jews, Palestinians, Christians, even Atheists, and it is not bound by one religion. Does that answer your question? (*He moves down to Naomi*)

Tariq Not really. In my book, Jews don't eat pork.
Naomi (*quietly*) I'm Jewish and I eat it.
Tariq You do? O.K. then, let's see you do it.

He holds out the roll but she declines it

Here, take it.
Naomi No.
Tariq Why not?
Naomi Because I am not hungry and I wouldn't touch anything after you had handled it.

Tariq is annoyed, he makes a slight movement towards her but Luis steps in between them. Tariq stares at him for a moment, he feels naked without his gun. He decides to bluff it out. He laughs, moving away left

Tariq Either way there is no point in wasting it. (*He bites off a huge mouthful and continues to speak as he chews*) Not bad, you do yourself all right, don't you?

Luis stares at him in silent disgust. Tariq decides to needle him. He goes to him a little, looking him up and down

I've often wondered about you fellows . . . with women I mean. Do you really go through life without a shake-down?

Luis turns away, right

I mean, you are a man, you've got feelings like other men and there must come a time when it's handed to you on a plate . . . I mean, some women get a kick out of being laid by someone like you. O.K. then, what do you do? Say "Sorry, but I'm not allowed" or do you give it a quick roll in the hay and pray afterwards? . . . Well, come on, you are a human being and sex is sex whatever clothes you wear.

Naomi appeals to Leila

Naomi (*pleading*) Stop him, please stop him.
Tariq (*aggressively*) Stop me? Why, what have I said? I just want to know. I mean I'm ignorant, he just said so, so why doesn't he tell me?

Leila is slightly amused by this, she turns to Luis

Leila It's a valid question, priest. Tell him.
Luis (*quietly*) Very well. I *am* human and suffer temptations like any other man.
Tariq (*insisting*) Yes, but do you give in?
Naomi (*a little hysterically*) Stop it, for God's sake, stop it.

She falls to her knees and buries her face in her hands despairingly. Tariq is about to carry on but changes his mind. He shrugs, then returns to his box and sits. He picks up a half-full bottle of cheap wine from the floor, pulls out the cork with his teeth then spits it out. Suddenly, as a gesture, he offers the bottle to Luis, who shakes his head. Tariq grins

Tariq You sly bastard, you wouldn't tell me anyway, would you?

(*He takes several gulps from the bottle, wipes his mouth with the back of his hand, then belches*) I'll give you Jews one thing, you make bloody good wine. (*He takes another swig*)

There is quite a pause

Naomi (*suddenly*) I want to go to the lavatory.
Leila (*curtly*) There is a bucket in the next room.
Naomi (*shocked*) A bucket!
Leila Yes, a bucket. (*She moves towards centre a little*) What the hell do you think this is, the goddam Hilton or something?

Naomi doesn't answer

Well?
Naomi (*quietly*) In the next room?
Leila In there. (*She indicates the door left with a slight movement of her head*)
Naomi (*quietly*) Thank you.

She is about to move when Leila speaks

Leila Go with her, Tariq.
Naomi (*shocked*) Not him!
Leila (*shortly*) It's him or nothing.
Naomi But not him . . . please . . . won't you come?
Leila (*viciously*) What's so special about you, anyway? Now make up your mind.

Naomi, near to tears, crosses slowly to the door left. Tariq, grinning, follows her down. At the door she turns and appeals once more to Leila

Naomi Please . . .

Leila turns her back on her

Tariq (*leering*) Do you want me to take you by the hand?

Naomi turns quickly and goes out. Tariq follows, laughing quietly

There is a long pause, then Luis speaks

Luis That was a despicable thing to do.

Leila gives him a short glance but does not answer

You seem to be an intelligent woman, does it give you pleasure to degrade the girl like that?
Leila (*quietly*) Since you ask . . . Yes.
Luis I don't believe that.
Leila (*curtly*) I don't give a damn what you believe.
Luis (*puzzled*) But why?
Leila In a way, it's a form of revenge.
Luis I don't understand.
Leila How could you, you don't know the circumstances. (*She appears lost in thought for a few moments*) My mother stepped on a land-mine left over from the Israeli war, she died instantly . . . my father lost his right leg in the same accident. My sister was just sixteen, three years older than me and between us we nursed my father . . . somehow . . . Nobody would help us and we had nothing coming in and were near to starvation. In desperation I nursed my father alone while my sister found a job to keep us all.
Luis (*quietly*) That was very commendable.

She turns on him, her voice rising

Leila Commendable! She took the only work available . . . she went into a brothel . . . a brothel frequented mostly by men from the local kibbutz. (*She pauses, frowning*) Now, every time I come into contact with someone like that girl out there, who has never known anything but luxury, I feel I

have to make them pay for every man of her class who has
defiled my sister's body. (*She pauses*) Does that make sense to
you now?

Luis (*quietly*) I didn't know, I'm sorry.

Leila You sounded as if you meant that.

Luis I do.

Leila How can you? How can you be sorry for me? I am holding you hostage, I may even have to kill you.

Luis (*quietly*) For the moment I had forgotten the circumstances.

*He sits on the box. She watches him curiously for a moment, then,
still covering him with her automatic, she crosses to him*

Leila You know, you interest me.

Luis In what way?

She moves above him down to his right as she speaks

Leila Oh, several things. To have walked in like you did means
you are one of three things, a fool, a sensation-seeker or a
brave man. Which is it, priest, tell me.

Luis (*simply*) I don't know. It was an impulse of the moment,
if I had hesitated I wouldn't have come.

Leila Usually I have little time for men, except to use them, but
there is a certain inner quality about you.

Luis There is nothing very special about me.

Leila Oh yes . . . take that business just now when Tariq was
baiting you about your sex life. Had it have been me I would
have gone for him, but you didn't, why?

Luis (*smiling*) Because it was meaningless as far as I am concerned. Chiefly because of my calling, that form of deviation
is never offered to me. Even prostitutes feel they are insulting
you if they were to offer themselves.

Leila You mean it's like . . . like spitting on a crucifix.

Luis Yes . . . yes, I suppose that is a simple way of putting it.
There is of course an even stronger argument against retalia-
tion and that is that you don't hit a man who is pointing a
machine-gun at you.

Leila You would only do it once with Tariq.

Luis Exactly . . . May I ask you something?

Leila What?

Luis You are basically a sensitive person.

Leila (*shortly*) Wrong. (*She moves above him to centre again*)

Luis Oh yes. If you weren't you wouldn't have spoken like that about your sister. That being so, what are you doing with someone like Tariq?

Leila In a job like this, isn't it obvious?

Luis Do you like him?

Leila I detest him but he is the best hit-man in our organization. He is devoid of any feelings and will kill without hesitation.

Luis (*quietly*) And you approve of that?

She is suddenly angry, she turns on him

Leila (*angrily*) Stop trying to make me feel guilty. This is a crusade and I'm just part of it. Always remember that somewhere along the line someone has to pay the price.

Luis (*a little forcefully*) That's a false argument and you——

Leila (*very curtly*) All right, priest, you've had your say.

He is about to speak again but lapses into silence

Leila Tell me something.

Luis If I can.

Leila Have you ever had sex?

Luis (*quietly*) Yes.

Leila (*smiling*) I'm glad, it makes me feel a little better.

Naomi enters followed by Tariq. She crosses to the sacks and kneels with her back to him. He moves centre, amused and turns to Luis

Tariq (*to Luis, grinning*) If you want to go, maybe she'll take you

He indicates Leila who ignores him. He goes back to his box, sits and casually lights a cigarette. After a moment Leila moves casually to Naomi to speak to her

Leila Is your husband in the city?

Naomi My husband died in a car crash three years ago, I live with my father now.

Leila What did you do before you were married . . . if anything?

Naomi I was a nurse in Tel Aviv.

If Leila is surprised she does not show it. She studies the girl for a moment before speaking

Leila Tell me about your children.
Naomi (*defensively*) What possible interest could that be to you?
Leila I merely asked because——

The buzzer on the telephone sounds. Tariq stands quickly and Leila moves across to the table and picks up the receiver. Both Luis and Naomi react to the tension

Yes. . . . Yes, I can hear you. . . . All right, put him on. (*She waits*) Yes, Minister, you have my terms, they are quite explicit. . . . Release Suleman Persha and the girl will come to no harm, it's as simple as that. . . . Well, it's up to you to convince the Israeli Government, then. . . . (*Angrily*) Look, I don't have to tell you your job, you have telex, radio and telephones and presumably you have somebody in authority to make the necessary decisions. (*She glances at her watch*) The time is now nearly six o'clock, you have twelve hours to come up with the answer. . . . What? . . . Very well, put him on. . . . (*She half-turns to Naomi*) It's your father.

Naomi stands

(*On the telephone*) Yes, Ambassador. . . . Your daughter is at the moment unharmed. . . . (*Angrily*) Why the hell should I lie to you? . . . Speak to her yourself.

She motions to Naomi who crosses in front of her and eagerly takes the telephone

Naomi Daddy? . . . (*Almost crying*) Oh Daddy. . . . Yes, I'm all right. . . . *Please* do as they say, get me out of here. . . . (*Pleading*) Please, I beg of you. . . .

Leila makes an attempt to take the telephone but Naomi turns away and won't give it up

(*To Leila*) No, no, not yet! (*On the telephone*) . . . Daddy? . . . (*Crying*) Kiss the kids for me. . . . Tell them . . . tell them——

Leila snatches the telephone from her and thrusts her away towards the sacks

Leila Get over there.
Naomi (*tearfully pleading*) Please let me talk to him some more.

Leila turns her back on her, Naomi goes to the sacks and kneels, weeping

Leila (*into the telephone*) Are you satisfied? It's up to you now.
. . . Look, I'm not concerned how you do it, you are the Ambassador, it's up to you to convince your Government that we mean business. . . . And remember, you have twelve hours. . . . Six o'clock tomorrow morning is the deadline.

She slams the telephone down. Tariq sits again on his box. Leila turns to the window and stares out. Luis goes to Naomi and half-kneeling puts a protective arm around her shoulders. She sobs pitifully as the Lights fade to a Black-out

INTRODUCE THEME MUSIC

SCENE 2

The same. The following morning at dawn

Tariq is apparently dozing in a sitting position. Naomi is stretched out on her stomach, sleeping, her head in her arms. Luis is sitting huddled on the box above the sacks. Leila, apparently relaxed, is gazing out of the window from which streams the early morning light. She glances at her watch then lights a cigarette

Luis (*quietly*) What's the time?
Leila A quarter to six.
Luis Have you slept at all?
Leila No.
Luis How long can you keep this up?
Leila As long as necessary. You didn't sleep much yourself.
Luis It was difficult with those searchlights trained on us.
Leila It's a two-edged sword.
Luis How do you mean?
Leila They want to be able to see us, but on the other hand we can see them, it is a safeguard against surprise attack.

Luis (*wearily*) I suppose. Is he asleep?

Leila No, and if you have any idea of trying to jump him he will shoot you before you have moved a couple of feet. Right, Tariq?

Tariq (*laconically*) Right, Leila.

She turns her back and gazes out of the window. There is a long pause

Leila (*softly*) There is something very beautiful about a city at sunrise.

Luis (*quietly, almost to himself*)
Earth has not anything to show more fair,
Dull would he be of soul who could pass by
A sight so touching in its majesty.
This city now doth like a garment wear
The beauty of the morning, silent, bare.

Leila turns and stares at him, frowning

(*Quietly*) Wordsworth . . . an English poet.

Leila (*curtly*) That decadent stuff has no place in my world.

Luis (*bitterly*) It wasn't written for people in your world.

Leila Meaning?

Luis It was written for those who love beauty as opposed to murder and destruction.

Leila You don't have a very good opinion of me.

Luis I despise you and everything you stand for.

Leila But you are not afraid of me?

Luis Oh yes I am, I know you wouldn't hesitate to kill me if you decided it was necessary.

Leila At least we understand each other on that. (*She turns away, apparently lost in thought*)

Luis What I don't understand is, what turns a girl like you into a barbaric terrorist.

Leila spins round on him, angry

Leila We are not terrorists, we are freedom fighters.

Luis (*angrily*) You are playing with words.

Leila (*forcefully*) No, we have a just cause and in case you have forgotten it, we are legitimate, we are now officially represented at the United Nations.

Luis Only because you have the backing of the Communist bloc.

Leila (*stubbornly*) To me this is a dedication.

Luis rises and moves left slightly, his voice betrays his emotion

Luis (*harshly*) Not a dedication, it's a way of life. (*He moves to her*) You revel in this, it's romantic. Right now the whole world is watching every movement on their T.V. sets, and you are the star performer. You are using the media for your own ego.

Leila (*moving to him a little*) And why not? Everything is justified if it stirs the concience of the world. Every time something like this happens we get a surge of new recruits.

Luis (*bitterly*) Yes, nine-year-old children trained by El Fatah. Most of them have never seen Palestine, many of them never will.

Leila Nevertheless, it strengthens our country.

Luis What you don't realize is that you are using the freedom of the media to destroy the freedom of the State which makes the media possible.

Leila You are talking in riddles. Tell me, priest, you call us terrorists?

Luis Yes.

Leila Right. How would you rate the generals who plotted to assassinate Hitler? By your rating they were terrorists too.

Luis They were brave men.

Leila They were prospective murderers.

Luis The issue was quite different, they were attempting to exterminate something evil.

Leila Whis is what we are trying to do. Drive out the people who have stolen our land. Have we no rights?

He breaks right a little as he speaks, almost in exasperation

Luis Everyone has rights, but you talk as if the whole country is behind you.

Leila (*curtly*) It is.

He moves a little towards her

Luis No. You are a minority group of fanatics. Hundreds of thousands of Palestinians live and work peacefully side by

side with the Israelis. The Israelis through sheer guts have
turned barren wastes into prosperity which your people never
knew before. (*He moves right as he speaks*) You can see it
wherever you go, cities, townships, vineyards, orange groves . . .
(*He turns to her*) And whatever your argument you can't deny
that your people have benefited by it.

Leila Only because they lacked the leadership to stand up for
themselves. That is what we are doing. That is our ultimate
goal.

Luis If you really believe that, you are sick . . . very sick.

Leila (*dangerously quiet*) Don't push me too far, priest.

They stare at each other for a moment then he speaks, quietly

Luis (*quietly*) What is your name?

Leila Leila.

Luis Leila . . . How can I convince you, Leila. (*He half-kneels
beside Naomi, placing a hand on her shoulder*) These are good
people. I know, I have worked beside them in a kibbutz
many times. Theirs is a world of construction, not destruction.

Leila Don't try and undermine my belief, for me this is my life,
my dedication, call it a death wish if you like because sooner
or later I shall not survive one of these raids.

Luis Even if you believe that, this isn't a woman's job.

Leila You don't understand, do you? An Arab woman is nothing to her own people, just something to kick around, unless
she can prove she is as good as a man or better. This is my
chance to prove to my people that I am worthy of them. If
I can secure the release of Suleman Persha no-one will ever
doubt my ability.

Luis And you would risk your life for a cold-blooded murderer
like him?

Leila He is a patriot, a brilliant strategist and a great leader.

Luis stands

Luis And you call a man who kills sixty innocent people, many
of them children, in an airport lounge with a machine-gun, a
great leader? You have got your values wrong.

She moves centre, annoyed

Leila Who are you to talk of values? (*She pauses, then moves to the box, places one foot on it resting easily with her arms on her leg. She goes on evenly*) Let me tell you something. I went to Jerusalem last year . . . your holy city. Holy! . . . You can't move for souvenir shops. Every American tourist takes back a piece of the original cross . . . by my reckoning it must have weighed about twenty tons . . . I thought I'd have a look at the place of your leader, so I called a taxi and said "Take me to Calvary", and do you know what he said? "I'll take you as far as I can, but it's a one-way street" . . . and you talk of values.

She moves back to the window and there is a pause. During this last scene Naomi has woken up and listened to their arguments

Naomi (*quietly*) Could I have some water?

Leila takes the bottle to the left end of the sacking and throws it with contempt beside Naomi. The girl looks at her for a moment then picks up the bottle and kneels, sitting on her feet. She pours some water out in her hand and rubs her face and neck with it gently. She then drinks a little and hands the bottle to Luis who also drinks. He hands the bottle to Leila who turns away abruptly

Leila (*curtly*) Keep it, I don't need any.

She returns to the table and Luis half-kneels beside Naomi

Luis (*to Naomi, gently*) Are you all right?
Leila (*curtly*) Of course she is all right, she has slept most of the night.
Naomi Has my father rung?

Tariq gives a sudden, coarse laugh

What is so funny?

Tariq gets up and comes down a little

Tariq You. "Has my father rung?". Where do you think you are, a bloody tennis club or something? (*Mimicking her*) "If he does ring, tell him I won't be home until late as I'm going to a dinner dance." (*He laughs again and moves down to the door left and turns*) Are you going to keep *me* company this time?

He coarsely unzips his flies. She turns away in disgust

   Laughing he goes out

There is a pause

Naomi (*quietly*) What is going to happen to us?
Leila That doesn't concern you.
Luis But it does. There is nothing we can do so is there any reason why we shouldn't know?
Leila I suppose not. The moment I hear of Persha's release we shall leave here.
Naomi How?
Leila We have hi-jacked a helicopter which will land on the roof here. It will take us to a small disused airfield well outside the city. We have a small executive jet waiting there with enough fuel to take us to Libya.
Naomi And then?
Leila When Persha is safely back you will be released.
Naomi And if they refuse to let him go?
Leila (*quietly*) I hope for your sake they make the right decision.

Naomi turns away and buries her face in her hands despairingly. Luis puts his arm round her to comfort her

Luis (*quietly*) It will be all right, I know it will.

Leila takes a small walkie-talkie set from the canvas bag. She pulls out the aerial then speaks quietly into it

Leila Come in, Ahmed . . . do you read me? (*She holds the set close to her ear then speaks into it again*) I am reading you faintly. . . . Stand by with the chopper from any time now. Out.

   She puts the set on the table as Tariq enters. Quickly, she spins round to cover him, but seeing who it is, relaxes

Tariq Ahmed?
Leila I've just told him to stand by.
Tariq How is he going to land? Every roof is crawling with snipers.

Leila I'll fix it when the time comes.
Tariq How?
Leila (*angrily*) Don't question my orders. I know what I am
  doing.

Her anger rouses him. He speaks angrily as he moves to his box

Tariq I wonder. What the hell does someone like you know
  about these things, they should have sent a man.
Leila (*almost shouting*) For the last time, Tariq——

He turns on her, shouting

Tariq You'll fix it? You don't realize what we are up against.
  (*Without realizing what he is doing he moves right into the
  opening left of his box in full view of the snipers. He points*)
  Have a look, they've got a bloody army down there, mortars,
  machine-guns, gas, the lot, and you, you stupid bitch, you
  say——

*There is a crack of a rifle shot and Tariq spins away right clutching
his upper left arm but still retaining his gun*

  Jesus!

*Leila rushes to him instinctively. She leaves her automatic on the
table*

Leila (*anxiously*) Are you all right, Tariq?
Tariq The bastard nicked me in the arm.

*As Tariq speaks, Luis seizes his opportunity and rushes to the table
snatching up Leila's automatic. Before he can even turn he is
covered by Tariq, who screams at him*

  Move and I'll cut you in half.

*Luis realizes that it is hopeless. He holds his hands above his
head*

  Put it back on the table . . . slowly.

Luis lowers the gun and lets it fall on to the table with a thud

  Now back away from it.

*Luis takes a few steps back. Leila moves to the table quickly and
snatches up her gun angrily. She points it at Luis*

Leila (*furiously*) Help him.
Luis (*bluntly*) No.
Leila I said, help him.

Luis turns his back on her and takes a step or so right. Leila is furious. She turns to Naomi

You! Come here.
Naomi (*stubbornly*) No.
Leila (*ice coldly*) If you want him to live, come here.

She deliberately points the gun at Luis' back. Naomi hesitates

I mean it.

Naomi moves to her slowly. Suddenly Leila snatches her wrist and spins her round. She thrusts her to the window pressing her gun into Naomi's face and using her body as a shield. She screams out of the window

Clear that roof . . . all of you, right now or I'll kill her . . . I mean it. I'll kill her!

She watches for a moment, then releases Naomi, who turns away sobbing. Tariq is sitting on the sacks nursing his arm and Leila thrusts Naomi towards him

You can earn your keep now. Fix him up.
Naomi (*sobbing*) How?
Leila You are a nurse, aren't you?
Naomi (*wildly*) But I haven't got anything.
Leila You've got a dress, haven't you, use a strip of that.

Naomi is nearly hysterical. She is about to try and make use of her dress then quickly takes off her half-slip. She tries to tear it down but it won't tear

Naomi (*hysterically*) It won't tear . . . it won't tear . . .
Tariq Bring it here.

She does so, holding it out

Hold it tight.

She holds it and he takes his knife and cuts down the material. He repeats this so that she has two strips of material about four

*inches wide. She kneels, facing upstage, and bandages his arm.
She has nearly finished when Tariq, with a grin, slips his hand under
her skirt and puts his hand on her thigh. She spins round angrily,
hitting him twice, as hard as she can, across the face*

Naomi You bastard . . . you filthy bastard . . .

Tariq (*grinning*) Don't flatter yourself, you are quite safe, I only
like them with big tits.

*Naomi sits facing upstage on the box, she hunches with the degrada-
tion of it all*

Leila O.K., Tariq?

Tariq Yes, it's only a nick.

Leila Right. Tell Shumac to get on the roof and wait for us,
there is plenty of cover under the parapet. When you have
done that come back here.

Tariq Right.

He goes out left

Leila picks up the walkie-talkie and speaks

Leila Do you read me, Ahmed? (*She listens with the set at her
ear*) O.K., bring the chopper in now. Out. (*She puts it down
and picks up the receiver of the field telephone, turns the handle
a few times, then listens*) Who is that? . . . Get me whoever is
in charge of security. . . . (*She waits*) Yes, I'm here. . . . Now
listen very carefully. . . . In a few minutes a chopper will be
landing on our roof. . . . If anyone fires at it on landing or
taking off we shall kill the girl without hesitation. . . . The
priest as well. . . . You understand? Good, make sure no-one
makes a mistake. (*She puts the receiver down and turns to
Luis, half-smiling*) Don't people like you pray at a time like
this?

Luis (*quietly*) If I were to it would not be for myself but for
you.

Leila There is no need, priest, no need at all. (*She glances at her
watch*) Any minute now we shall get the news of Persha's
release, then we shall all have a pleasant flight, we might even
toast our success in champagne. In a few days' time you can
sell your story to the press.

Tariq returns

Tariq (*grudgingly*) I don't know how you did it but all the snipers have left the roofs and it's all clear.
Leila Good. How is your arm?
Tariq Hurting, but I'll live. How many does the chopper hold?
Leila Four and the pilot.
Tariq There are five of us including Shumac.
Leila Yes.
Tariq So who stays behind?
Leila That's an interesting question.
Tariq There are three of us and the girl.
Leila Which leaves the priest.
Naomi (*quickly*) You can't kill him.
Leila No? Do you expect me to kill one of my own men?

Naomi gets up quickly, pleading

Naomi But you can't, he came here of his own free will to try and save me, you can't murder him . . . you can't.
Leila I do however admire his guts in coming here and in fact there is no need to kill him. He can remain here unharmed when we leave. (*She turns to Luis, smiling*) Would you accept that as a generous gesture from a freedom fighter, priest?

He does not answer

Or would you prefer that I was a terrorist and shot you?

The sound of the helicopter is heard as it approaches

Tariq Here is Ahmed now.

After a moment there is a dull thud as it lands on the roof

He's made it.

Suddenly the buzzer sounds from the telephone. Leila snatches up the receiver

Leila Yes? . . . Yes. . . . (*She frowns*) You realize what you are saying? . . . Yes. . . . (*Angrily*) Yes, I understand. (*She slams the telephone down furiously*)
Tariq What?

Leila turns to Naomi

Leila (*furiously*) You will be interested to know that your Israeli cabinet sat all night and have decided that they will not bargain. They say that as an Israeli you must expect to die for your country.

Naomi, shocked, turns to Luis, who puts his arms round her protectively

Naomi (*quietly*) Oh God . . . Oh God, no.

Luis (*harshly*) You lost. I told you you can't underrate these people.

Leila (*shouting*) Stop preaching at me. (*To Naomi*) And to think that I shall be condemned for failure over someone like *you*.

Naomi (*pleading tearfully*) Please . . . please, I beg of you . . . please . . .

Leila (*curtly*) Take her out, Tariq. You know what to do.

Tariq Right. Come on.

He moves across and snatches Naomi from Luis

Naomi (*wildly*) Where are you taking me?

Tariq Out.

Naomi (*almost screaming*) What are you going to do?

Tariq Come on.

Luis makes a movement to help her but is covered by Leila

Luis (*shouting*) No, no, for God's sake no.

Leila (*shouting*) Keep out of this.

Naomi is screaming hysterically as Tariq thrusts her out left

Luis (*pleading*) Stop him while there is still time. For God's sake, show a little mercy.

Leila (*shouting*) Mercy! With someone like that?

Naomi (*off*) No, No . . . oh please——

There is the sound of a shot followed by a piercing scream followed by two more shots. Leila, momentarily distracted, half turns to the door. Luis, seizing his chance, hurls himself. He manages to grab her gun and taking her arm spin her round. They struggle for a moment then he thrusts her away from him towards the sacks where she sprawls. He moves across to above and behind her, standing over her with the gun, shaking. He speaks with barely controlled emotion

Luis You murderer, you cold-blooded murderer . . . you killed her without any compunction or mercy . . . you couldn't even bring yourself to do it, you let an animal like Tariq do your filthy work for you. Can you think of any reason why you shouldn't die too?

Leila (*quietly*) No. All you have to do is to pull the trigger. You see, priest, I am not afraid to die . . . it's like I said, a kind of death wish . . . Even if we are lucky enough not to be shot down in the chopper, my own people will kill me for failing . . . so . . . what does it matter if you pull the trigger?

He deliberately points the gun at her head, his hand shaking visibly. He stands for a few seconds, almost transfixed, but his conscience will not let him go through with it. He lowers his arm and with his head bowed sinks on to one knee, looking away from her. She rises quickly, takes the gun from his unresisting hand, then goes to the table. She thrusts the walkie-talkie and the radio into the bag and at this moment Tariq appears

Tariq enters

Tariq What now?
Leila We get out as fast as we can.
Tariq What about him?
Leila (*shortly*) Leave him.
Tariq Are you crazy?
Leila (*sharply*) I said leave him.
Tariq Like hell.

He raises his gun and shoots Luis twice. Luis reels under the impact, clutches his chest and half collapses in a kneeling position

Tariq Come on, let's get to hell out of here.

Tariq exits quickly

Leila gathers up the bag and her gun and strides to the door. She stops, then turns, looking at Luis

Leila (*softly*) It seems we both lost, priest.

She turns abruptly and goes out

Luis, after a moment, summons enough strength to stagger to the table. He waits a few seconds to regain his strength then picks up the telephone

Luis Hello . . . hello . . . Why don't you answer, for God's sake . . . hello. (*He realizes that he has not activated the call signal. He winds the small handle on the side with difficulty*) Hello. . . . Yes. . . . Listen, they—— . . . Never mind that, *listen* to me. . . . They have shot the girl. . . . She's dead. . . . They are alone in the helicopter. . . . Shoot them down, kill them. (*Shouting*) Kill them . . . kill them . . .! (*He slips to the floor and the receiver falls from his hand. He is suddenly horrified at his own action, he sinks to his knees, his hands clasped he looks up in prayer. He cries as he speaks*) Oh God, forgive me . . . *please* . . . I beg of you . . . forgive me. (*He makes an attempt to cross himself but collapses as he does so*)

CURTAIN

FURNITURE AND PROPERTY LIST

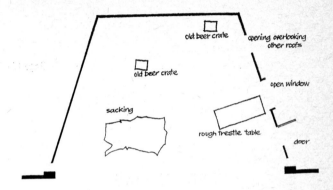

On stage: Dirty sacks
Two wooden crates
Small trestle table. *On it:* army water-bottle, small transistor
radio, small canvas satchel. *In satchel:* walkie-talkie radio
and hand-grenade
General rubbish
Bottle of cheap wine

Off stage: Field telephone on light wire

Personal: **Tariq:** sub-machine gun
Leila: gun, watch, cigarettes
Luis: small linen roll containing meat rolls

LIGHTING PLOT

Property fittings: nil

SCENE 1

To open: General lighting

Cue 1   **Naomi** sobs   (Page 18)
         Black-out

SCENE 2

To open: Dawn light

No cues

EFFECTS PLOT

SCENE 1

Cue 1   As CURTAIN rises   (Page 1)
         Music plays

Cue 2   **Leila** switches off radio   (Page 2)
         Music stops

Cue 3   **Leila** replaces grenade on table   (Page 6)
         Empty tin rattling

Cue 4   Lights fade to Black-out   (Page 18)
         Introduce theme music

SCENE 2

Cue 5   **Leila:** ". . . was a terrorist and shot you?"   (Page 27)
         Helicopter approaches

Cue 6   **Tariq:** "Here is Ahmed now."   (Page 27)
         Dull thud on roof

Cue 7   **Tariq:** "He's made it."   (Page 27)
         Telephone buzzer